SMALL BUSINESS IDEAS FOR ASPIRING ENTREPRENEURS

Series 1

JERRY L PRICE

Small Business Ideas for the Aspiring Entrepreneur

Jerry L Price

Small Business Ideas for the Aspiring Entrepreneur

Small Business Ideas Series #1

Starting a Small Business
Being an Entrepreneur

Landscaping or Curb Appeal Company
Hot Dog Business During Annual Sporting Events
Moving Company
Snow Cone Business & Festivals
Gourmet Apples Online Business
Cleaning Service Business
Marketing & Promotion Online Business

Starting A Small Business

Small Business Ideas for the Aspiring Entrepreneur is a great book for individuals looking to supplement their income on a part-time or full-time basis, or someone looking to venture out and start a business within 6-12 months.

Starting a small business isn't that hard at all. The hard part is actually convincing yourself that you have the ability to be successful. The rewards you get from your own efforts by far surpass anything you could imagine.

From idea to the first customer, every decision you make as a small business owner will yield an outcome; and from that outcome, you will decide how to strategically position your company to become a market leader and generate more revenue than your competitors.

Let's challenge the status quo by living up to our potential. This resources guide will outline business opportunities all around us and highlight marketing and branding strategies that can be used to turn a potential lead into a satisfying customer.

Being an Entrepreneur

Being an entrepreneur means that you have the ability to see opportunity in everything. Your primary objective as an entrepreneur is to find ways in which your talent or expertise will aid you in generating income for yourself.

This book will teach you the difference between a brand and a product, and identify ways in which you can diversify a product line that is already successful.

Everywhere you look, business deals are being made. From negotiating the price of a car, to negotiating your salary, you were born to be an entrepreneur. Your desire to cut costs and retain your income would equate to cutting overhead costs to retain profits.

Nothing is easy. However if you apply the same energy you use to be productive at your current job, you will without a doubt be successful. It will take a few failures and countless tries along the way, but once you get it, the rest is up-hill from there.

My objective is to help you identify and leverage your core competencies around limited resources to build a small business. Be it part time or full time, starting a small business using the skills you currently have can supplement your income and can improve your life style significantly.

Starting a Landscaping or Curb Appeal Company
Chapter 1

Small Business Ideas For Aspiring Entrepreneur

Landscaping & Curb Appeal Business Idea**

Projected Startup Costs: Part Time ($280-$500) Full Time ($2,500 -$5,000)
Sales Revenue: Residential Part Time ($480-$1,200) | Commercial ($3,000-$6,000)

Over the past decade, the landscaping sector has increased significantly due to the number participants in this particular market space. As noted by NFIB.com, "the U.S. landscaping industry **nets $61 billion** annually according to the Professional Land care Network (Planet) a national group that represents landscape contractors and lawn-care specialist." As demand for lawn care services increase, so does the opportunity to make substantial revenue as a small business owner.

In this chapter we will assess the opportunities, costs, and potential revenue you can make as a landscaping professional. To begin, lets say you live on a block that has **12** houses and each house has a <u>front</u> and <u>back</u> lawn.

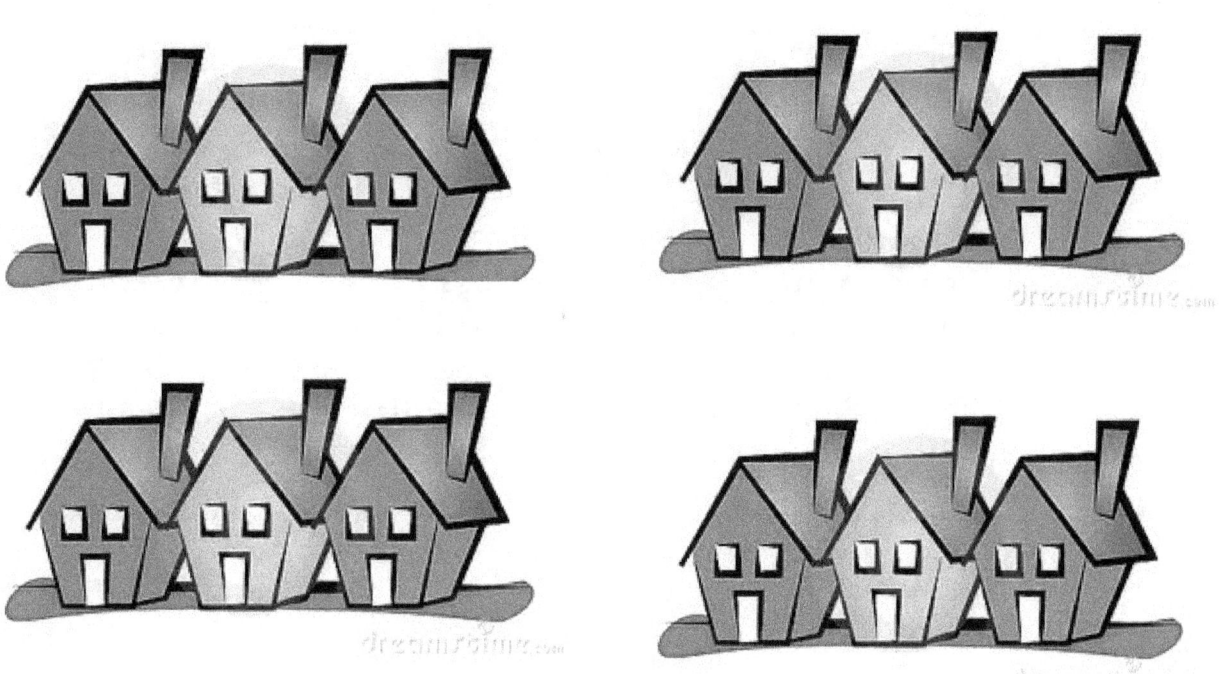

Now lets say you charge each homeowner **$40.00** to cut their <u>front</u> and <u>back</u> lawns plus trim and clean up. That is **$40.00** per house times the number of houses on the block which is $480.00.

Small Business Ideas For Aspiring Entrepreneur

$40.00 * 12 (number of houses) = $480.00

As I recall, grass grows every 2 weeks so that means you will have to service block's lawn twice a month. Now remember this is only 1 block, imagine if it were 10 blocks or more.

$480.00 * 2 (twice a month) = $960.00 revenue.

Now that you see the potential sales revenue you can generate from owning your own landscaping business, let's look at the initial start-up costs.

To start a small **residential** landscaping business you would need:
- **1-2** lawn mowers depending on the lawn size
- 1-2 portable electric grass trimmers
- Hefty Garbage Bags 58 pack
- 1-2 grass rakes
- 1 gas can

Start-Up Costs & Business Expenses

Equipment	Cost for 1	Cost for 2
Lawn Mowers	$185.15	$370.30
Grass Trimmer	$56.60	$113.20
Hefty Garbage Bags 58 pack	$22.10	$44.20
Rakes	$10.98	$21.96
Gas Can	$22.89	$45.78
Total Investment	$297.72	$595.44

Prices represent the <u>average</u> cost you can expect to pay for each.

Now if you decide to start off by purchasing only **1** of each ($297.72) you will make a return on your investment within the first 2 weeks if you service 12 homes. Remember the example above?

Small Business Ideas For Aspiring Entrepreneur

Lets continue to use those financial projections to see the potential profit you can obtain from this venture.

Service Revenue	Cost Per Home	12 homes
Lawn Mowers Service	$40.00	**$480.00**

Equipment Expenses		**Costs for 1 of Each**
Lawn Mowers Business		$297.72

Total Return On Investment		$182.28

If you do **24** lawns a month, that is **288** lawns a year. Multiple **288** by **$40.00** (your service fee) you have the potential to make $11,520.00 a year just cutting grass (before expenses).

If you live in states that have a number of seasons you can be sure to diversify your services to include:

- Autumn Leaf Removal Service **$20-$30.00**
- Snow Removal and Salting Pavement **$50.00-$80.00**

Note to Entrepreneur

The landscaping business is an annual demand that can yield substantial profit margins for anyone looking to participate in this market segment. The projected figures outlined within this chapter only account for **residential** households. Now imagine, if you will, the amount of revenue that can be obtained by contracting for commercial real estate developments or private properties.
Start off by doing what you can. The revenue you obtain from servicing residential properties can be re-invested into your business to purchase commercial equipment that will double your ROI and profits.

Business Fact

In certain areas, having a lawn care business can generate well over half a million dollars a year if you market and brand your company effectively. You can become the best lawn-care provider in your area by simply offering better services, a professional presentation, productive staff and administrative personnel, and better price points than your competitors.

Things you will need to build a better brand:

- Website
- 800 Business Number & Automated Answering Service
- Order Forms or Invoices
- Small Business Certifications (vary per state)
- EIN number to open a business account
- Professional Slacks, Logo, and Shirts
- Business Cards/ Flyers/ Door Hangers

Starting a Hot Dog Business During Annual Sporting Events

Chapter 2

Small Business Ideas For Aspiring Entrepreneur

Hot Dog Business During Annual Sporting Events

Projected Startup Costs: Part Time ($280-$500) Full Time ($2,500 -$5,000)
Sales Revenue: Residential Part Time ($480-$1,200) | Commercial ($3,000-$6,000)

Starting a hot dog vending business during annual sporting events can be a very good business idea. Think of it this way, every year in every state there are hundreds of sporting events that take place. *(You can obtain a list of all annual sporting events from your local Chamber of Commerce, city hall, or county.)* This business opportunity is relatively easy to start. For example, in Chicago IL alone we have:

Little League		**Track & Field**
Baseball	12-25 games	Ages 7-13
Softball	8-15 games	
Football	15-40 games	
Soccer	15-25 games	

High School		**Track & Field**
Baseball	12-25 games	Ages 14-18
Softball	8-15 games	
Football	15-40 games	
Soccer	15-25 games	

Every sporting event varies per city and includes both male/female athletic events.

Lets look at the potential revenue starting with a **Little League** baseball game for boys. During a normal season, **1 team** plays around **20 teams**. At a preseason game there may be 20-30 parents & family members and 12-15 kids playing per team.

Small Business Ideas For Aspiring Entrepreneur

That is on average about 40-50 potential customers. Knowing that, you price your products accordingly:

Hog Dog **$2.00**
Chips **$1.00**
Water or Soft Drink **$1.00**

Baseball Meal Deal **$5.00**
Hot dog, Chips, Soft Drink

Now lets say during this same game, **15** kids brought your "**Baseball Meal Deal** for **$5.00**, **10** kids brought just a **hot dog & soft drink**, and **5** parents just brought a **bottle of water**. Your total potential revenue would be:

    Baseball Meal Deal $75.00
    Hot Dog & Soft Drink $30.00
    Water $5.00

  Total Revenue for 1 game: **$110.00**

  Total Revenue for 20 games: **$2,200**

Given that every game occurs on Saturday and Sundays between 9:00am-3:00pm; this business opportunity can be a great source of income.

If I can recall, some park districts will host a number of games on the same day. On an average, there can be somewhere between 4 games a day at a park district. If you set up a central location where potential customers can see you, you can make around $400-$600 daily. Multiply that by 20 games a season that is $8,000-$12,000.00.

Small Business Ideas For Aspiring Entrepreneur

To start a small **Hot Dog Vending business** during annual sporting events you would need to:

- Rent or Purchase Mobile Vending Cart
- Vendors License
- Park/Vending permits
- Find food stores to purchase food products

Start-Up Costs & Business Expenses

Equipment	Cost
Hot Dog Push Cart	$1,999.00
20 Packs of Hot Dogs $4.58 a pack	$91.60
20 packs of Hot Dog Buns $5.00	$100.00
2 Ketchup & Mustard Squirt Bottles	$25.16
500 Hot Dog Trays	$15.98
1 Bottle Water Bulk	$12.25
3 Can Soda Bulk	$15.00

Total Investment $2,258.99

Prices represent the <u>average</u> cost you can expect to pay for each.

If it cost $2,258.99 to start this business you will have to sell 452 Hot Dog Deals (Hot Dog, Chips and Soda or Water) to break even and get your return on your investment.

You can do it!

Small Business Ideas For Aspiring Entrepreneur

Note to Entrepreneur

Starting a weekend hot dog vending service can be fun, entertaining and lucrative at the same time. The numbers of annual sporting events vary per city so be sure to get your list of events from your local chamber of commerce.

Business Fact

Deciding to start a weekend Hot Dog vending business can be very lucrative. All you have to do is purchase the items listed above, get your professional vending state licenses, and find out what sporting events will be taking place in your area by contacting your chamber of commerce department. It's that simple.

Things you will need to build a better brand:

- Website
- State Vending Licenses
- EIN number to open a business account
- Professional Slacks, Logo, and Shirts
- Business Cards/ Flyers

Starting a Moving Company

Chapter 3

Small Business Ideas For Aspiring Entrepreneur

Moving Company Business Idea**

Projected Startup Costs: Part Time ($4,455.60) Full Time ($8,911.20-$10,995.00)
Sales Revenue: Residential Part Time ($14,250.00) | Commercial ($28,500) 6 months

Every year millions of Americans have to deal with the headache of moving from one residential area to another. The stress of having to pack your possessions, find and rent the right size moving truck, load and unload the boxes, plus put gas back into the rental truck can be extremely difficult for some and a pain for others.

Not only is moving difficult at times, it is frustrating if you find out that the moving truck you rented has been leased out by another party.

In this chapter, we will explore the opportunities of starting and maintaining a small business moving company. To start, here are the business parameters.

Start Up:
Finance or Purchase Moving Truck
Create Website
Marketing Materials & Door Hangers
Monthly Coupon Packages*

Business Operations:
$55-$65 per person for 1 hour (minimum 2 movers)
Truck Rental Fee **$90.00** (gas expense paid by customer)
Minimum 3.5 Hours
50% deposit needed to reserve moving date

Brand Savings & Expansion:
Monthly Repair Savings is **10%** of Retained Revenue after Expenses
Expand within **2-3** years to include commercial Rates

Small Business Ideas For Aspiring Entrepreneur

Start-Up

As outlined in the start-up section, to start a moving business your major purchases would be:

- Financing or Purchasing Moving Truck
  - Creating Website
  - Marketing Materials Door Hangers
  - Monthly Coupon Packages

In order to increase brand awareness and marketing I would advise using Groupon™, partnering with local apartment complexes, partnering with neighborhood clubs, etc *

Equipment	Cost
Moving Truck Financing	$3,995.00
Create Website +Hosting	$210.60
Marketing Material To Start	$250.00
Official 1-800 Number + Fax Number*	$38.00 monthly *
Temporary Email Account*	FREE
Total Estimated Investment	$4,455.60

Items listed with the (*) simply means you can wait to purchase those items until your sales revenue increase. Also the **Moving Truck** rate does not include taxes or finance chargers. Everything listed is just a projected estimate and is subject to change. The total estimated investment amount listed does not include the $38.00 monthly telephone number charge.

Places to Buy Moving Trucks:

- http://www.uhaul.com/TruckSales/
- http://www.commercialtrucktrader.com/
- http://www.penskeusedtrucks.com/
- https://www.budgettruck.com/buytrucks.aspx

Small Business Ideas For Aspiring Entrepreneur

Now that you know the start-up projected costs for a small moving business lets now look at the potential revenue.

Business Operations:
- **$55-$65** per person for 1 hour (minimum 2 movers)
- Truck Rental Fee **$90.00** (gas expense paid by customer)
- Minimum 3.5 Hours
- **50%** deposit needed to reserve moving date

To start, if you charge a customer **$110.00** per hour for 2 movers (*$55 per mover*), a truck rental fee of **$90.00** for a minimum of **3.5 hours** plus a **50%** deposit your projected revenue for one move would be as follows:

$110.00 * 3.5 hour = $385.00 moving fee
$385.00 moving fee + $90.00 truck rental = $475.00 sales revenue
50% required to Book Appointment = $237.50

Recap:

2 movers for 3.5 hours @ $55 per person and truck rental fee $90.00

$385.00 moving fee

$385.00 moving fee + $90.00 truck rental = $475.00 sales revenue

50% required to Book Appointment = $237.50

If your new moving company successfully complete **5 moves** a month during the moving season; within **6 months** that's a total of 30 moves

30 moves * $475.00 (2 movers +$90.00 truck rental for 3.5 hours) = **$14,250.00 sales revenue**

This means that within 6 months you have successfully made a **ROI** (return on investment).

Small Business Ideas For Aspiring Entrepreneur

Sales Revenue $14,250.00

Total Estimated Investment:	**$4,455.60**
Total Net After Start Up Expenses:	**$9,794.40**

If you make $9,794.34 within 6 months, you can set aside **10%** ($979.43) to go towards truck maintenance which leaves $8,814.91

Now before you raise the initial investment, please be sure to obtain the list of required items below:

- Contact your State Commerce Commission's office for proper certifications
- Offer Free Written Estimates of the probable cost of the move
- Obtain Carrier's Liability Insurance
- Packing and Loading Pre-Preparation Training for employees
- Delivery Receipt Booklet
- Payment Due Before uploading Begins unless charged already
- Develop A Refund/ Cancellations Policy
- Develop Intrastate Vs Interstate Move Policy

Note to Entrepreneur

Starting a moving company may require the acquisition of a moving truck to great started, but the profit margins overtime is worth the investment.

Small Business Ideas For Aspiring Entrepreneur

Snow Cone Business & Festivals

Chapter 4

Small Business Ideas For Aspiring Entrepreneur

Snow Cone Business & Festivals**

Projected Startup Costs: Part Time ($3,519.04) Full Time ($12,107.04- $15,685.04)
Sales Revenue: Residential Part Time ($4,219.04) | Commercial ($28,500) 6 months

Starting a snow cone business on a part time or full time basis can generate modest revenue during an annual festival. If you reside in a state that's hot annually you can turn this part-time business into a lucrative career.

To start a mobile snow cone business you will need a few items:

- Snow Cone Professional Mobile Cart
- Snow Cone Ice Shaver
- Flavor Station
- Branded Cups
- Straws
- Large Bags of Ice
- Foam Ice Cooler & Scoop

Equipment Part-Time	Cost
Snow Cone Professional Mobile Cart	$943.25
Snow Cone Ice Shaver*	$589.00
Flavor Station*	$1100.00
Mobile Generator	$480.00
2000 Foam Cups & Straws	$68.00
3 Foam Ice Cooler & Scoop	$320.00
8 Large Bags of Ice	$2.38 per bag
Part Time Total Estimated Investment	$3,519.04

Small Business Ideas For Aspiring Entrepreneur

Equipment Full-Time	Cost
Snow Cone Professional Mobile Cart	$6,760.00
2 Snow Cone Ice Shaver	$3,360.00
Flavor Station	$1,100.00
Mobile Generator	$480.00
Branded Cups & Straws	$68.00
Foam Ice Cooler & Scoop	$320.00
Large Bags of Ice	$2.38 per bag
Full Time Total Estimated Investment	$12,107.04

Places to Purchase Equipment:

- http://allacart.com/
- http://www.snowie.com/
- http://www.ebay.com/
- http://www.1-800-shaved-ice.com/shiceandsnco3.html

Now that you know the start-up projected costs for a small snow cone business lets now look at the potential revenue.

Business Operation & Pricing:

Small Cup	$3.00
Medium Cup	$5.00
Large Cup	$7.00

Now say that you paid $700.00 to participate during an annual festival in your city. The $700.00 vending fee gives you the opportunity to vend for **3** consecutive days. If the festival attracts on average **25,000** people per day, you project that the festival will attract in total **75,000** guests.

Small Business Ideas For Aspiring Entrepreneur

If out of the **75,000** expected guests only **8%** of them purchase your medium snow cone cup @ $5.00 per cup you would make $30,000.00 in one weekend.

75,000 guests * .08 = **6000** guests
6,000 guests * **$5.00** Medium Snow Cone Cup = $30,000.00

Sales Revenue Example $30,000.00	
Part Time Investment:	$3,519.04+ $700 *vending fee*
Full Time Investment:	$12,107.04+ $700 *vending fee*

If you make $30,000.00 during the weekend festival as described above, you would have made a return on your investment (part-time or full-time) plus retained profits by attending only 1 festival.

$30,000.00 - $4,219.04 (Part-Time Investment) = $25,780.96
$30,000.00 - $12,807.04 (Full-Time Investment) = $17,192.96

The revenue listed does not take into consideration that you will have to purchase more ice to serve 6000 people. It only estimates that you will make a ROI (return on your investment) if you attend the weekend festival and 6000 people purchase your medium cups at $5.00 per snow cone

Now before you raise the initial investment, please be sure to obtain the list of required items below:

- Contact your State Commerce Commission's office for proper certifications
- Research Annual Festivals in your State and/or City
- Purchase a POS system or Payment Processing System
- Purchase Flavors in advance as they have a long storage life
- Optional: Develop a Professional Website or Social Media Page

As you can see, starting a snow cone mobile business and partaking in annual festivals can be a very lucrative endeavor.

Small Business Ideas For Aspiring Entrepreneur

Gourmet Apples Online Business
Chapter 5

Small Business Ideas For Aspiring Entrepreneur

Gourmet Apples Online Business**

Projected Startup Costs: Part Time ($2,464.25-$3,500.00) Full Time (11,014.25$- $15K)
Sales Revenue: Online Part Time ($5,182.65) | Commercial ($10,365.30) 6 months

Gourmet apples aren't just a delicious treat, they can be a great starting point for an aspiring entrepreneur looking to starting their own online business.

To start an online gourmet apple business you will need a few items:

- Website / Unique Brand Name
- Apple Supplier
- Caramel Supplies
- Heating Tray
- 800 Number & Email
- Social Media Marketing Strategy
- Professional Brand Packaging

Equipment Part-Time	Cost
Website + Domain Name + Web Hosting 1 year	$250.00
Apple Supplier (Local Fresh Food Market)*	$38.95 *a pound*
Caramel Commercial Supplies & Equipment *	$1100.00
Caramel Warming Trays & Appliances	$614.25
Professional Brand Packaging	$500.00
Social Media Marketing Strategy	FREE Networks

Part Time Total Estimated Investment $2,464.25

Total does not include the number of apples you will purchase

Caramel commercial supplies consist of the caramel dipping sauce and supplies needed to make the caramel.

Small Business Ideas For Aspiring Entrepreneur

Equipment Full-Time	Cost
Website + Domain Name + Web Hosting 5 year	$500.00
Apple Supplier (Local Fresh Food Market)*	$38.95 a pound
Caramel Commercial Supplier Equipment *	$3500.00
Caramel Warming Trays & Appliances	$614.25
Professional Brand Packaging	$500.00
Small Store Front Rent for 6 months lease	$4,200.00
Professional Licenses & Certifications	$600.00
Store Front Marketing Material & Supplies	$1,100.00
Social Media Marketing Strategy	FREE Networks
Full Time Total Estimated Investment	$11,014.25

Total does not include the number of apples you will purchase

Places to Purchase Equipment:

- http://www.gmpopcorn.com/products/product-sections.cfm?catid=17
- http://www.jarcoindustries.com/CandyApples.htm

Now that you know the start-up projected costs for a small snow cone business lets now look at the potential revenue.

Sample Business Operation & Pricing:

Gourmet Apples	$3.95
4 Apples Package	$15.80
1 Dozen Gourmet Apples	$47.40
Gourmet Basket	$30.00

Small Business Ideas For Aspiring Entrepreneur

Before you start making your gourmet delicious treats and selling them online, you have to take into the account the shelf-life of your products.

The shelf-life for gourmet apples is **2-3** days. This means you have to sale your gourmet apples within that time frame or risk bad inventory.

This is what we know, selling your gourmet apples online will allow you to reach more customers. Knowing you have 2-3 days to sell your products reduce wasted inventory because you will only produce apples based on purchase orders.

Now that you understand the fundamentals of starting an online gourmet apple business, lets now look at the numbers. Say you decided to launch your business in February; a week before Valentine's day; given the amount of traffic converted from your social media page, let's say your business produced these projected financial results in the first 2 months:

	Price	Customers	Total
1 Gourmet Apple	$3.95	25	$98.75
4 Apples Package	$15.80	50	$790.00
1 Dozen Gourmet Apples	$47.40	12	$568.80
Gourmet Basket	$30.00	9	$270.00
			$1,727.55

If you generate $1,727.55 in sales revenue you can project that within 3 months you will break-even as a part-time merchant and break-even in 6-8 months as a full-time merchant.

$1,727.55 part-time sales revenue * 3 months = **$5,182.65**
$1,727.55 full-time sales revenue * 6 months = **$10,365.30**

Start-up Expense	
Part Time Investment:	$2,464.25
Full Time Investment:	$11,014.25

Small Business Ideas For Aspiring Entrepreneur

The revenue listed does not take into consideration the number of apples needed to complete the order, packaging and delivery. It only outlines that you will make a ROI (return on your investment) if you commit to generating the average number of sales listed

Now before you raise the initial investment, please be sure to obtain the list of required items below:

- Contact your State Commerce Commission's office for proper certifications
- Research your competition
- Purchase a POS system or Payment Processing System
- Purchase a number of caramel containers and caramel sticks
- Develop a Professional Website and Social Media Page
- Boost every post on your social media page
- Purchase ads on google ad words.

Small Business Ideas For Aspiring Entrepreneur

Cleaning Service Business
Chapter 6

Cleaning Service Business**
Projected Startup Costs: Part Time ($4,106--$4,500.00) Full Time (15,814.25$- $17K)
Sales Revenue: Online Part Time ($6,000.00) | Commercial ($10,000.00-$20,000.00)

Deciding to start a cleaning business can be very lucrative given the amount of real estate (commercial and residential) that need constant cleaning for presentation purposes.

Property owners hire cleaning services for a number of reasons. They may need to vacant unit or property cleaned for an upcoming open house or the investment maintained overtime. Whatever the reason, this can be a great business opportunity for aspiring entrepreneurs.

To start a Cleaning business you will need a few items:

- Website / Unique Brand Name
- Cleaning Supplies
- Compensation Contracts
- 800 Number & Email
- Social Media Marketing Strategy

Small Business Ideas For Aspiring Entrepreneur

- Professional Brand Packaging

Equipment Full-Time	Cost
Website + Domain Name + Web Hosting 5 year	$500.00
Cleaning Supplies & Uniforms	$4,600.00
Cleaning Supply Equipment *	$3,500.00
Temp Contactors Monthly	$814.25
Professional Brand Packaging	$500.00
Small Store Front Rent for 6 months lease	$4,200.00
PT/FT Employees $8.00 per hour	$50-$160 per week
Professional Licenses & Certifications	$600.00
Store Front Marketing Material & Supplies	$1,100.00
Social Media Marketing Strategy	FREE Networks
Full Time Total Estimated Investment	$15,814.25

Equipment Part-Time	Cost
Website + Domain Name + Web Hosting 1 year	$250.00
Cleaning Supplies & Uniforms	$2,800.00
Professional Compensation Contracts	$100.00
800 Number-$38.00 per month	$456.00 Annually
Professional Brand Packaging	$500.00
Part-Time Temp Employees $8.00 per hour	$50-$160 per week
Social Media Marketing Strategy	FREE Networks
Part Time Total Estimated Investment	$4,106.00

Total Investment does not include the number of supplies you will purchase or the number of hours a temporary employee will work

Total does not include the number of supplies you will purchase

Small Business Ideas For Aspiring Entrepreneur

Places to Purchase Equipment:

- http://www.restockit.com/cleaning-supplies/floor-cleaning/
- http://www.bjs.com/breakroom--maintenance/cleaning-products

Now that you know the start-up projected costs for a cleaning service business lets now look at the potential revenue.

Sample Business Operation & Pricing:

$35 per hour room
$70 per hour for 2 rooms
$105.00 per hour for 3 rooms plus

Monthly Charge

$125.00-$250.00 Single Family Property
$500.00- $1,500.00 Commercial Property Vacant

Given the pricing structure outlined, lets say you successfully acquired 5 contracts due to your awesome marketing strategy. The potential revenue results are outlined below:

3 Single Family Contacts	$250.00 per month/ 6 months	**$1,500.00**
1 Commercial Property	$500.00 per month/ 3 months	**$1,500.00**
1 service request	$70.00 per hour/ 4 hours total	**$280.00**
Total Projected Sales Revenue (before expenses):		**$3,280.00**

Now that you understand the fundamentals of starting a cleaning business, lets focus on the growth potential. If the 3 single family home customers and the owner of the commercial property listed above requested to renew their services for 12 months. Your projected financial sales revenue before expenses would be:

3 Single Family Contracts

Small Business Ideas For Aspiring Entrepreneur

$3,000.00 / ($250.00 * 12 months)

1 Commercial Property
$3,000.00 / ($250.00 * 12 months)

Total Sales Projection: **$6,000.00**

The revenue listed does not take into consideration the number of supplies and employees needed to complete the service request. It only outlines that you will make a ROI (return on your investment) if you commit to generating the average number of sales listed for 2 years

Now before you raise the initial investment, please be sure to obtain the list of required items below:

- Contact your State Commerce Commission's office for proper certifications
- Research your competition
- Create a list of commercial property clients within your area
- Purchase a POS system or Payment Processing System
- Develop a Professional Website and Social Media Page
- Boost every post on your social media page
- Purchase ads on google ad words.
- Go out there and market your brand!

Small Business Ideas For Aspiring Entrepreneur

Small Business Ideas For Aspiring Entrepreneur

Starting A Marketing & Promotions Online Business

Chapter 7

Starting A Marketing & Promotions Online Business**

Projected Startup Costs: Part Time ($1,406.00-$2,500.00) Full Time ($8,000)
Sales Revenue: Online Part Time ($24,620.00) | Commercial ($49,240.00) 6 months

Starting an online marketing and promotions firm is the best way to ensure a great return on your investment within 6-12 months. This business generally has low overhead and start-up costs. Your ability to effectively utilize social media by converting "likes" to "sales" and directing "potential customers" to your website using hyperlinks can generate substantial income.

To start an Online Marketing Firm you will need a few items:

- Website / Unique Brand Name
- Marketing Material
- 800 Number & Email Account
- Social Media Marketing Strategy
- Professional Brand Packaging

Small Business Ideas For Aspiring Entrepreneur

- E-Blast Account Holder
- Social Media Pages

Equipment Full-Time	Cost
Website + Domain Name + Web Hosting 5 year	$250.00
Professional Marketing Material/ Flyers	$600.00
Professional Contract Forms/ Invoices	$500.00
Temp Social Media Team Monthly	$800.00
Professional E-Blast Account $25.00 per month	$300.00 Annually
Small Store Front Rent for 6 months lease	$4,200.00
Professional Licenses & Certifications	$600.00
Store Front Marketing Material & Supplies	$1,100.00
Social Media pages	FREE Networks
Full Time Total Estimated Investment	$8,350.00

Equipment Part-Time	Cost
Website + Domain Name + Web Hosting 1 year	$250.00
Professional Marketing Material/ Flyers	$300.00
Professional Contract Forms	$100.00
800 Number-$38.00 per month	$456.00 Annually
Professional E-Blast Account $25.00 per month	$300.00 Annually
Social Media Pages	FREE Networks
Part Time Total Estimated Investment	$1,406.00

Total does not include the number of supplies you will purchase

Small Business Ideas For Aspiring Entrepreneur

Places to Purchase Equipment:

- www.wix.com (website)
- www.godaddy.com (purchase domain name)
- Set up Social Media Pages
- Paypal Account, Cube Square, Point of Sale System
- http://www.vistaprint.com/?GP=11%2f19%2f2014+10%3a53%3a15+AM&GPS=3341298631&GNF=0

Now that you know the start-up projected costs for an online marketing and promotions firm business lets now look at the potential revenue.

As a social media marketing firm you can offer your potential clients a number of service packages. Here is a few:

Sample Business Operation & Pricing:

E-Blasting Clients (Flyers, Business Links, Promotion Material)

    2 months/ 10 e-blasts $250.00
    3 months/ 15 e-blasts $380.00
    5 months/ 25 e-blasts $450.00
    6 months/ 30 e-blasts $560.00

Social Media Marketing and Promotion for Clients

$200.00 per month/ small business
$500.00 per month/ midsize firms
$1,500.00+ per month/ large firms with over 30 employees

Small Business Ideas For Aspiring Entrepreneur

For this service you will manage their social media pages

Now lets say a small flower shop hired you to do their social media marketing and promotion for **6 months** leading up to the valentine's day weekend. You would offer this customer:

6 months/ 30 e-blasts $560.00

$200.00 per month/ small business = $1,200.00

Total Potential Sales Revenue: **$1,760.00**

In 6 months you have the potential to generate $1,760.00. What if you are able to successfully acquire **12 small business accounts** and **5 midsize accounts** your projected sales revenue using the same example will be:

12 small business accounts:
$21,120.00

5 midsize business accounts
$3,500.00

Total Sales Revenue for **6 month** Contract:
$24,620.00

Marketing firms have low overhead coast and their inventory is usually zero. Majority of their content is stored as digital files and cost

Small Business Ideas For Aspiring Entrepreneur

nothing to forward to clients. In this business, you potential earning potential can be significant.

Now before you raise the initial investment, please be sure to obtain the list of required items below:

- Contact your State Commerce Commission's office for proper certifications
- Research your competition
- Create a list of potential clients within your area
- Set up a Paypal account or Payment Processing System
- Develop a Professional Website and Social Media Page
- Boost every post on your social media page
- Purchase ads on google ad words.
- Go out there and market your brand!

If you need professional consultation to start or expand your business, please follow utilize the resources below:

https://www.sba.gov/

https://www.sba.gov/category/navigation-structure/starting-managing-business

https://www.sba.gov/content/what-sba-offers-help-small-businesses-grow

https://www.sba.gov/tools/local-assistance/regionaloffices

https://www.score.org/

SBEI | Small Business Entrepreneur Initiative

Email: SBEIGlobal@yahoo.com

Social Media Link: https://www.facebook.com/SBEI4U
Temporary Website: http://sbei52.wix.com/sbei

Small Business Ideas For Aspiring Entrepreneur

Consultant:
Jerry L Price, MBA
Office: (312) 898-2831

This business book contains forward-looking statements regarding projected future results.

Forward-looking statements include all statements that do not relate solely to historical or current facts, and generally can be identified by the use of words such as "may," "believe," "will," "expect," "project," "estimate," "anticipate," "plan," "could," "would," "likely," "intend" or "continue." All forward-looking statements are inherently uncertain as they are based on various expectations and assumptions concerning future events and are subject to numerous known and unknown risks and uncertainties which could cause actual events or results to differ materially from those projected.

Small Business Ideas For Aspiring Entrepreneur